Douglas Somerset
18th Feb 1989

THE

BRAVE BOYS OF DERRY;

OR,

NO SURRENDER.

By W. STANLEY MARTIN,

Eaitor of "Uncle Ben's Budget," and Author of "Some Famous Bonfires";
"Fireships, Fireworks, and Firebrands"; "The Man who Fought
the Giants"; "The Tinker of Bedford and the Book
that he Wrote"; "Turn or Burn"; etc.

MOURNE MISSIONARY TRUST
4, Church Road, Carginagh
Kilkeel, Co. Down
N. Ireland BT34 4QB.
Tel. (06937) 62248
1986

D1395791

The writer hopes that, with God's blessing, this little effort may do something to foster in the hearts of his young readers a similar spirit to that which filled the breasts of the apprentice boys of Londonderry when they shut the gates of the city in the face of the Pope's army, and that they too will be found standing firm, and, if need be, suffering joyfully in the cause of truth and freedom.

PREFACE.

THE thrilling story of the Siege of London-derry will never be forgotten by all true Protestants and lovers of liberty. It forms one of those episodes of the past which the boys and girls of the present should know somewhat of, because, although it is a story of the long ago, it is full of lessons for the present.

The following pages are only of an elementary nature, and are purposely written in a simple style so that its readers will have a story to peruse and not a history lesson imposed upon them after school hours.

To all his readers the author urges the reading of the charming pages of Lord Macaulay's " History of England," which has now, happily, been issued at a price within the reach of all.

THE BRAVE BOYS OF DERRY.

CHAPTER I.

England's Back-door.

I N a former book[*] I told you the story of how King James II. was sent about his business because he tried to again bring England under the power of Romanism.

But though James ran away as quickly as ever he could, when he found that the Prince of Orange was actually on his track, he did not by any means give up the hope of returning once again to the shores of old England, to try once more to accomplish his knavish tricks.

It would have been very easy for the Prince of Orange and his supporters to have put James in prison, and let him feel the strong arm of the law that he had so despised; but there can be little doubt they did not want

[*] "Fireships, Fireworks, and Firebrands," by W. Stanley Martin,

the trouble of disposing of another trouble-
some Stuart king in the same manner as
Charles I. had been dealt with, so they gave
him every opportunity to escape. And so one
dark night away he went to France, to his
dear friend Louis XIV., and these two
worthies were soon plotting and planning
the downfall of England, and especially the
uprooting of England's Protestantism.

Now I must explain to you that James,
though lacking in common sense, was by no
means lacking in a shrewd sort of cunning,
and he had foreseen the possibility of events
turning out as they had done. He had therefore during the few years of his reign arranged
that in Ireland at least, the reins of govern-
ment should be in the hands of his supporters.

When James came to the throne there was
a Protestant Lord Lieutenant in Ireland; but
he was promptly dismissed and the Roman
Catholic Earl of Tyrconnell (or "lying Dick
Talbot" as he was generally called) put in his
place. That gentleman soon made his in-
fluence felt; every Englishman was turned out
of office. Every Judge, every Privy Coun-
cillor, every Mayor and Alderman of a
borough was required to be a Romanist and
an Irishman. All the Protestants in the
army in Ireland were turned out of it, and at
the time of James's flight it consisted of no
less than fifty thousand men, all pledged to
the restoration of James to the English
throne, and with it the restoration of Romanism in our country.

King William the Third, the Prince of Orange.

So you see, although James was turned out of the front door in England, he hoped to gain an entrance once more by the back door. The back door was Ireland, and to that "distressful country," he with the help of Louis was soon speeding his way, and arrived there in due course. He was accompanied by a number of French officers, who were to do their best to reduce the wild hordes of the Irish to a disciplined army, and to teach them the polite manners practised in France. We shall see later on what these manners of polite French society were like.

The journey to Dublin was not exactly the sort one would choose for an holiday jaunt. The country was a desert. What should have been fruitful fields was a long stretch of devastation. Horses were most difficult to procure. But the enthusiasm of the inhabitants was unbounded. They effusively welcomed the man whom they expected to be their deliverer from Protestant tyranny; but from the records that exist of that memorable journey, it does not seem to have impressed the English ex-king or his French officers very favourably. The crowds of Irish were wild in their aspect, and their manners were not of the nicest. They meant well, no doubt, but when garlands in which cabbage stalks were the prominent feature were offered to the kingly deliverer, it was rather trying to his sense of humour if he had any. When, however, the Irish women insisted on kissing James the

"The enthusiasm of the inhabitants was unbounded."

limit was reached, and he ordered his body guard to keep them at a distance.

At length, after much discomfort and with considerable disgust at the uncouth manners of his new friends, James arrived at Dublin. After staying there for a little while he continued his journey towards the north, where the brave inhabitants of Londonderry were making what preparation they could for a prolonged siege. The journey was an utterly miserable one, the country he passed through being a very wilderness; what was not devastated was bog, rock, or wild, bleak moorland; and to add to the misery a prolonged storm of rain and wind fought against the advancing monarch. At length Londonderry was reached, and his army was found encamped a few miles to the south of the city, under the command of a General Hamilton. The French officers with James declared that it was impossible for the city to hold out, and that at the sight of an organised army they would no doubt open their gates and accept whatever terms were offered them; but Hamilton, who knew more of what sort of stuff they were made of, thought otherwise. He knew that the majority of the men within the town were sturdy Protestants, who never knew when they were beaten. We shall find that General Hamilton was correct in his estimate of the sort of men he had to deal with.

CHAPTER II.

"Bring a Great Gun This Way."

ND now, having brought the ex-King James to the gates of Londonderry, I must tell you how matters had fared with the Protestants of the north of Ireland up to this time. When it became known that James was intending to wage war against England and Protestantism, using Ireland as his point of attack, it was soon noticed that on all sides the Irish Roman Catholic peasantry were laying in stores of pikes and knives, and the priests from a thousand so-called altars were preaching death to the Protestants, and reminding the poor ignorant people of the wrath of God which King Saul brought upon himself for sparing the lives of the Amalekites. Little wonder, then, that the Protestants of Ulster—who were mostly of Scotch and English extraction—industrious and God-fearing men and women, many of whose parents had suffered for their steadfastness to the truth of God, felt concerned about their own safety, especially when it was known that all the power was in the hands of blood-thirsty men who were looking forward to the near approach of the time when the hated and envied Protestants were to be put to the sword, and their property divided among themselves.

Throughout the country, for weeks, Protestants in outlying districts were being insulted, their houses set on fire and their cattle killed, and, in many cases, their persons attacked. Everything seemed to be at boiling point when it was whispered from mouth to mouth and from hamlet to hamlet that on December 9th, 1688, a general massacre of the Protestants was to take place.

On the side of the Protestants every mansion was strengthened, and from all sides, wherever it was possible, they gathered together to defend themselves against their foes, who, inflamed by their priests, would stop at nothing.

In the north of Ireland, in Ulster, large numbers of the Protestants took refuge within the walls of the city of Londonderry, on the Foyle. From all sides they crowded in, expecting to find temporary safety, at least, from their foes. But soon a new danger arose. " Lying Dick Talbot " had done his master's bidding well, and had taken care that the principal officers in the large towns were followers of King James. It was thus in Londonderry. Although the people were for resisting the Irish, the corporation of the town were not at all inclined to adopt such a course. Therefore, when the news arrived that a regiment of 1200 Romanists, under the command of the Earl of Antrim,

"They rushed to the Ferry Gate, and closed it in the face of the King's Officers, shouting as they did so, 'No Surrender!'"

was marching nearer every minute to take possession, great was the consternation. Some were for closing the gates and resisting, others for submitting.

The destiny of thousands of Protestants was in the balance. Even the Bishop of Londonderry—a Protestant, but I expect one of the milk and water sort—was for opening the gates to King James's army. He looked upon James as the Lord's anointed king, and therefore it would be wrong to be found opposing him. In the meanwhile, the Earl of Antrim was drawing nearer and nearer. A company of his army arrived at the gate and demanded admittance in the name of King James. But while the negotiations were going on, there were in the town a large number who were very indignant at the turn things were taking. They knew that whatever promises might be made them upon surrendering, they would be broken, as the understanding was then, as it is now, in the Romish ranks, "that no faith was to be kept with heretics." Among those who were about boiling over with wrath were thirteen young men, only apprentices, but apparently sharp as needles and as quick as swallows, for, while the terms of surrender were being discussed, they ran in a body to the guard-room, seized the keys of the city gates, rushed to the Ferry Gate, closed it in the face of the King's officers, and let down the portcullis, shouting as they did so, "No surrender! No surrender!" But this was not all. Now the young blood had started the business, older hands took the matter up, and a man named James Morrison mounted the walls, and in pretty plain terms told the intruders that they had better make themselves scarce. But still they hesitated. They had been told to take possession of the town, and had been led to suppose that there would not be any real opposition, and here they were, baffled by a handful of apprentice boys. They began to hold a consultation, but old Morrison, still standing on the walls and looking back into the city, shouted out, " Bring a great gun this way." *That* settled the matter ; the big gun argument was unanswerable, and the enemy retreated to a place of safety on the other side of the river.

Inside the city all was stir and bustle ; the action of the apprentice lads had been like a spark to a barrel of gunpowder. The whole city was up. The gauntlet had been thrown down, and it was now to be a fight ; and we shall see what a terrible business it meant. All the other gates were made secure ; sentinels paced the ramparts ; muskets and ammunition were served out ; and during the night messengers were speeding their way to the Protestant gentry in the locality who had not yet come to the city, to come and bring all the help they could. The poor Bishop was terribly upset. He pointed out what a terrible thing it was to be found fighting against their lawful sovereign ; just as if when their lives were at stake they were to tamely

"Bring a big gun this way."

lick the dust before their enemies. Besides this, King James had been sent to the right-about in England by those who knew more about James's tricks than, I suspect, did the Bishop. On one occasion the worthy man was preaching a sermon on the usual lines when he was interrupted by one of the apprentices by, "A good sermon, my lord; a very good sermon; but we have not time to hear it just now." It was not at all good manners, but I expect it expressed the feelings of the bulk of the inhabitants very well indeed. However, we will say good-bye to poor Bishop Hopkins; he had soon had enough of Londonderry and its fiery apprentices, and he shortly afterwards left the city and travelled to London, so we need not trouble ourselves any more about him.

"A good sermon, my lord; a very good sermon; but we have not time to hear it just now."

CHAPTER III.

"An Enemy Within the Gates."

THE city was never intended for a siege; the fortifications consisted simply of a wall overgrown with grass and weeds; there was no ditch, even, before the gates; the draw-bridges had long been neglected; the chains were rusty and could hardly be used, and, to add to the danger, on the outside of the town were heights admirably suited for planting guns upon, so that cannon balls could easily be fired into the town. But this was not all, for even if the garrison could defend itself against the experienced generals who accompanied James, they would soon discover that one of their worst enemies would prove to be starvation, for their stock of provisions was very small, and now that the inhabitants of the town had increased to over eight fold, it looked as if their position was indeed a desperate one.

But one of the greatest dangers was that some of the inhabitants were in league with the enemy; there were traitors in the town; and you know a secret enemy within the gates is far more dangerous than an open enemy outside. The Governor of the city was a Colonel named Lundy, and it was strongly suspected that he was only waiting his opportunity to hand over the keys of the garrison to the enemy. He did all he possibly could to discourage those who were for holding out to the end. He said that resistance was useless, and that they had better make the best terms they could with James while they had the chance. What the end would have been I do not know, but just at this time the hearts of all the loyalists were gladdened by seeing some English war ships in the bay. They contained two regiments of soldiers which had been sent from England to reinforce the garrison. But such a proceeding was not at all to the mind of the traitor Colonel Lundy, so he assured their commander that resistance was hopeless and that he had better take his soldiers back again to England. A council of war was held, but good care was taken that only those who were at one with Lundy were invited; but even in this packed council there was one brave soldier, who protested that to " give up Londonderry was to give up Ireland," but all the thanks he received was contemptuous abuse.

After this little bit of treachery had been satisfactorily arranged, the miserable traitor Lundy privately sent a messenger to the headquarters of the enemy, telling them that they could depend upon the garrison surrendering when the formal demand was made. But this was not to be; Protestants were not thus to be sold to their worst foes; God had better things in store for the north of Ireland than that, although it was to mean terrible suffering for those who were to keep the grand flag of "No surrender" flying. When the news of what had passed in the council was whispered in the streets the indignation of the soldiers and the inhabitants knew no bounds. Some were for shooting the traitor, and others said that the scoundrel should be hanged upon the walls of the city. It was noticed, too, that those most in the confidence of Lundy were sneaking out of town whenever they had the chance; and then, to crown it all, on the evening of April 17th, 1689, it was found that the gates of the town had been opened and that the keys had mysteriously disappeared. The guards were doubled and the pass words changed, and an attack was expected every minute, but nothing occurred. When the day dawned a meeting of the principal inhabitants was held. It was a stormy meeting; Lundy was told that he had sold the town to its worst enemy, and that he deserved hanging. While the discussion was at its height, a shout was heard from the ramparts, and it was found that the vanguard of the enemy's army was in sight and that James himself was with it to demand admission. Lundy ordered that there should be no firing, but his authority was at an end. Two brave soldiers, Captain Baker and

" Ships had been sighted on Lough Foyle."

Captain Murray called the inhabitants to arms, and in this they were nobly assisted by an aged minister named the Rev. George Walker, the Rector of Donaghmore, who, with many of his neighbours, had taken refuge in Londonderry. Remember this good man's name, for he, under God, was the means of untold good to the noble defenders of the city, as we shall see as we go on. There was now a tremendous stir within the city; the menfolk rushed to the walls and manned the guns, and when they looked out beyond the city there was James within a hundred yards of them. But no sooner was he recognised than there arose a mighty shout of, " No surrender ! " and bang went one of the guns, and an officer standing at James's side fell dead. This was not at all the reception that he expected, so he and his attendants made their bow, and departed as quickly as their legs could carry them.

The traitor Lundy was now in a pretty tight corner, I can tell you. It was not safe for him to show himself, for fear of being torn limb from limb ; he therefore hid himself in some out-of-the-way corner, and when night came, having disguised himself as a porter, he managed to effect his escape. Murray and Walker knew all about this little plan, but they winked at it, as they did not want the disagreeable business of hanging him, and he would be less harm outside the walls than inside; so away he went, and we need not trouble our heads about him any more as we have to tell of better, braver and nobler men than men of the stamp of Colonel Lundy. In Londonderry to-day his effigy is annually burnt with every mark of disgust that can be bestowed upon an effigy.

Escape of Colonel Lundy.

CHAPTER IV.

"No Surrender!"

AND now the terrible business began in earnest. Two Governors were elected in the place of the traitor Lundy; one was Captain Baker, and the other was the Rev. George Walker, the aged Rector of Donagh- more. His especial work was to look after the distribution of ammunition, and also to see that tranquility was maintained within the town. Everybody respected the venerable minister, who proved himself to be not only a man of God, but also a brave soldier—in fact, a real old ironside. The provisions were also given out in regular rations, so that they might last as long as possible. But with this arrangement there was also the equally necessary arrangements made for united and constant prayer; and so it soon fell out that while in the enemy's camp there was drunkenness and profanity, there was within the walls prayer constantly ascending to the God of battles. Church of England and Nonconformist ministers vied with one another in cheering the inhabitants and leading in prayer and worship. The cathe- dral, where all met for prayer, was used partly as a place for worship and partly as a battery—for on the roof were planted some guns, while down in the vaults were stored quantities of ammunition. Thus, while there was without all that was disturbing, there was at the same time harmony and unity of purpose in the hearts of the defenders.

The walls and gates of the town looked feeble enough to the besiegers, so it was not long before a battering ram was thundering against one of the gates. The guns roared, the balls whistled through the air, and soon the town was on fire in several places, and many of the inhabitants, to whom the realities of war were before unknown, were alarmed to see roofs crashing in, houses falling, and many victims claimed in what proved to be but the beginning of their sufferings.

But familiarity with danger and death only had the effect of emboldening the inhabitants. No thought of giving in entered their heads, but, on the contrary, they assumed the offensive, and on April 21st a sally was arranged, and from the city streamed a sturdy little army determined to carry the conflict into the enemy's camp. It was under the command of Murray. A fierce conflict followed; a French general was slain, and 200 of the Irish were killed and wounded before the besieged were driven again into the city. Murray was nearly killed; his horse was slain and he was surrounded by soldiers, but he gave a good account of himself until his dangerous position was noticed by old Walker, the minister, who dashed out from the city with several armed men, and it was not long before those who had counted Murray as their victim were scampering away as quickly as their legs could carry them.

May arrived, and still the besieged held out, and still the besieging army continued to wonder how it was that they were unable to force an entrance, or why the despised inhabitants behind their antiquated fortifications could show such a stubborn resistance. During this month another early morning sally was made, which was as successful as the first, as another French general was mortally wounded, and among the trophies of war exhibited in the cathedral were two French banners, torn from the besiegers after desperate fighting. Many sallies and skirmishes now took place, but so intrepid were the besieged that the French and Irish troops began to consider as to whether some other method had not better be attempted to reduce the garrison to the submission which had been expected so long before. It was, however, decided to make one more huge effort to take the city.

A number of the most desperate characters in James' army bound themselves together by an oath to force themselves into the city or to perish in the attempt. It was decided to attack an outwork called Windmill Hill, which was not far from the southern gate. The attack was led by a Captain Butler. No

"The conflict soon waged furiously."

secret was apparently made of their purpose, for the Irish came on with an awful roar, and it was soon seen that it was a case of death or glory with a vengeance ; but they soon found that a warm welcome had been prepared for them, for the walls were manned with determined men in ranks three deep.   The front rank were armed with firearms, and kept up a continual fusillade, while the duty of those in the second and third was to take the place of any who fell, as well as to keep the front rank supplied with firearms and ammunition.   The conflict soon waged furiously.   At one time, where the wall was only seven feet high, Butler and his men succeeded in reaching the top, but without avail, as every one of them were either slain or taken prisoner.   At length, when about four hundred of them had been left dead, wounded or prisoners, the retreat sounded, and the discomfited remnant retired as best they could.

Great was the gratitude within the walls, and it was felt that no small part of the success was due to the noble women of Londonderry, who, in the thickest of the fight, had kept the men supplied with water, and had also helped in dealing out the ammunition.

It was now clear that the city was not to be taken by assault.   Other means must be tried.

It was not only the enemy outside the walls that the brave defenders had to contend with ;

remorseless foes, in the shape of hunger and fever, came to the aid of the Irish, and it was now evident that the besieged would have to be starved out of their position. The most extraordinary means were adopted to prevent any food being taken into the town. All down the river banks were forts and batteries to prevent any ships with relief on board making their way to the city; and then, in order to make assurance doubly sure, a boom, or barricade, was cast right across the river about a mile and a half below the city. This is how it was made; several boats full of stones were sunk, a row of stakes was driven into the bottom of the river, and then right across huge beams of wood were placed, joined together, and at either end, by stout cables, the formidable obstruction was made fast to the shores. Thus it seemed that the last hope of the brave inhabitants of Londonderry was extinguished. They strained their eyes in vain to see the welcome sails of a relieving force from England in the distant waters of Lough Foyle. And even if a vessel arrived it would prove no easy task to run the gauntlet of the forts and then to force the boom, all the while under the fire from the shore.

In the meanwhile in England the noble defenders of Londonderry had not been forgotten, but there had been many delays caused by the critical state of the country, for William III. had only just ascended the throne, and there were many other matters that required all the attention of the King and his Parliament.   At length in the English Parliament some of the members began to get impatient at the delay in relieving the Protestants in the north of Ireland, and one member got up and in a very warm speech said, " This is no time for counting cost.   Are those brave fellows in Londonderry to be deserted ?   If we lose them, will not the world cry shame on us ? A boom across the river !   Why have we not cut the boom in pieces ?   Are our brethren to perish almost in sight of England, within a few hours of our shores ? "   The people began to stir in the matter, and while a large army was being fitted out to be sent to cope with James in Ireland, a special relief force was despatched under General Kirke.   He sailed on May 26th, but contrary winds made his progress very slow, so we will leave Kirke's ships battling with the winds and waves of the Irish Sea, and will see how the heroic defenders within the city were faring as that long summer wore on.

CHAPTER V.

" Relief at Last."

THE distress had now become extreme. Hollow faces and sunken eyes were to be seen on all sides. Food was becoming very scarce. Horses were being eaten, but with the utmost care, as their supply was very limited. With the meagre supply of horseflesh was doled out tallow, but this too was becoming very scarce.

On June 15th the long deferred hope of the starving multitude was raised, for the sentinel on the lookout on the cathedral reported that ships had been sighted away on the blue sea in Lough Foyle. There they were, thirty vessels in all, and it was seen that they were signalling to the town, but their signals could not be made out. Surely the time of trial and suffering was now nigh over and relief was at hand. The vessels cast anchor in the bay and the townsfolk waited. How long the hours appeared to be. Would they never attack the enemy's position and arrive in triumph at the quay ? At last a messenger, with his life in his hand, made his way from the fleet to the town. He eluded the Irish sentinels, he dived under the boom, and informed the garrison that the fleet was under the command of Kirke, and that on board the ships there was an abundant supply, not only of ammunition, but what was so sorely needed, provisions that would satisfy many hungry mouths. Great was the excitement. Relief was at hand. The terrible waiting and suffering was all but over. Brighter days were awaiting them. But their hopes were doomed to bitter disappointment. Weeks of utter misery were to follow. Kirke, for some reason or other, thought it unsafe to make any attempt at relief for the present, and retired to the entrance of Lough Foyle, where he lay inactive for several weeks. The time may have not appeared to have been long on the ships, but in the city, affairs were getting worse every day. Every nook and cranny in every house was searched out in the hope that some secret supply of food might be found, and here and there, stowed away in cellars and garrets, such secret stores were discovered and carried away to go into the common stock. Cannon balls were, too, almost all used up, but in their place stones were covered with lead and were promptly despatched to the enemy's quarters, for still in the midst of their terrible sufferings the idea of surrender was never for a moment entertained. Fever was now daily carrying off its scores. But in the midst of all their woe, united prayer ascended to God, and trustful hearts still relied upon His aid, and looked for the time when by His help their calamities would be overpast. Walker, the brave minister, was ever in their midst, now cheering the cast down, now preaching words of hope, and then with sword in hand withstanding an assault from the enemy, showing that he was as good a soldier as he was a minister of the Word.

James, who was at Dublin, heard that ships had arrived to relieve the besieged city, and thought that if the city was not soon compelled to give in it would be too late; so a fresh move was made. The command of the besieging force was given to a French soldier named Marshal Rosen, who was not only a great soldier, but a most terrible ruffian. He was past feeling, and would stick at nothing to accomplish his purpose, so no sooner did he arrive before the walls than he made some tremendous efforts to settle the matter out of hand. He tried to undermine the walls so as to blow them up, and thus make a breach into which he and his followers could rush and soon put the inhabitants to the sword, but it was no good. The enemy were too alert for him, and after a sharp fight he had to retire with the loss of a hundred men. His rage then knew no bounds. What, was he, a marshal of France, an old soldier, who knew all there was to be known about the most approved method of scientific warfare, to be baffled by a herd of shopkeepers and farmers behind a wall that would be the laughing-stock of any properly trained soldier ? He would show them what he was made of, and make them bitterly repent the opposition they were showing. His rage was terrible. He would raze the city to the ground—everybody should be slain. Not a baby should be left alive ; and as for the men, he would put them on the rack, aye, he would roast them alive, and as a first instalment he caused a shell to be sent into the city with a terrible threat attached to it. It was this. He would send out on all sides and gather together all the Protestants who had not left their homes, mostly old men and women and children, he would then drive them under the walls of the city, and then, in sight of the inhabitants, starve them to death, besides exposing them to whatever weather might come. It was no idle threat. At the point of the sword crowds of poor helpless old folk (too old and feeble to bear arms), accompanied by numbers of little boys and girls, many of whose parents were within the city, were driven under the walls. It was indeed a pitiable sight and must have been a terrible one to the poor people within the city. Rosen thought that such cruelty would accomplish what fair warfare could not do, but again he was mistaken. He had yet to learn of what sort of stuff the inhabitants were made of. His cruelty would quell the spirits of the defenders thought he, but the only effect it had was to make them more determined than ever. An order was issued that within the city no one was to utter the word "surrender" under pain of death, and nobody uttered the forbidden word. But Rosen was not to have it all his own way, for there were within the city many very distinguished prisoners of war, who had up till then been treated as well as possible, but now they were to be used as a weapon against the oppressor. A gallows was erected on the walls, and a message was sent to Rosen to send a priest to prepare the prisoners for death as they were to be hanged like traitors if the poor creatures now huddled under the walls were not immediately released. The prisoners also sent a message, begging that their lives might be spared from such an end. After a delay, and only just in time to spare the prisoners' necks, Rosen relented and permitted the poor wretches under the walls to depart, but it was not before many had perished through exposure. The gallows was then taken down.

" By this time July was far advanced, and the state of the city was hour by hour becoming more frightful. The number of the inhabitants had been thinned more by famine and disease than by the fire of the enemy. Yet that fire was sharper and more constant than ever. One of the gates was beaten in, one of the bastions was laid in ruins; but the breaches made by day were repaired by night with indefatigable activity. Every attack was still repelled. But the fighting men of the garrison were so much exhausted that they could scarcely keep their legs. Several of them, in the act of striking at the enemy, fell down from mere weakness. A very small quantity of grain remained, and was doled out by mouthfuls. The stock of salted hides was considerable, and by gnawing them the garrison appeased the rage of hunger. Dogs, fattened on the blood of the slain, who lay unburied round the town, were luxuries which few could afford to purchase. The price of a whelp's paw was five shillings and sixpence. Nine horses were still alive, and but barely alive. They were so lean that little meat was likely to be found upon them. It was, however, determined to slaughter them for food. The people perished so fast, that it was impossible for the survivors to perform the rites of sepulture. There was scarcely a cellar in which some corpse was not decaying. Such was the extremity of distress, that the rats who came to feast in these hideous dens were eagerly hunted and greedily devoured. A small fish, caught in the river, was too precious to be purchased with money. The only price for which such a treasure could be obtained was some handfuls of oatmeal. Leprosies, such as strange and unwholesome diet engenders, made existence a constant torment. The whole city was poisoned by the stench exhaled from the bodies of the dead and of the half dead. That there should be fits of discontent and insubordination among men enduring such misery was inevitable. At one moment it was suspected that Walker had laid up somewhere a secret store of food, and was revelling in private, while he exhorted others to suffer resolutely for the good cause. His

"The attack on the boom."

house was strictly examined : his innocence was
fully proved : he regained his popularity ; and
the garrison, with death in near prospect,
thronged to the cathedral to hear him preach,
drank in his earnest eloquence with delight,
and went forth from the house of God with
haggard faces and tottering steps, but with
spirit still unsubdued.   There were, indeed,
some secret plottings.   A very few obscure
traitors opened communications with the
enemy.   But it was necessary that all such
dealings should be carefully concealed.   None
dared to utter publicly any words, save words
of defiance and stubborn resolution.   Even in
that extremity the general cry was 'No
surrender.'   And there were not wanting
voices, which in low tones added, " First the
horses and hides, and then the prisoners, and
then each other."   It was afterwards related,
half in jest, yet not without a horrible mixture
of earnest, that a corpulent citizen, whose
bulk presented a strange contrast to the
skeletons which surrounded him, thought it ex-
pedient to conceal himself from the numerous
eyes which followed him with cannibal looks
whenever he appeared in the streets."*

And all the while there, within sight of the
starving multitudes, were to be seen the vessels
that had been sent to relieve them ; there they
were, at anchor in the lough, and on board
were the abundant supplies that were so sorely
needed.   Many were the attempts that were

---

* Lord Macaulay.

made to communicate with the garrison, but most of them were without success. One brave man who attempted to dive under the boom was drowned, and another was captured and ignominiously hanged. At length a letter, sewed up in a button, reached Walker from Kirke, assuring the brave governor that relief would now be speedy. Great was the expectation. Surely their sufferings were now all but over; it was impossible for them to hold out more than two days longer, but they did, for another weary fortnight dragged on, and still the city was not relieved. About this time Kirke received positive orders to relieve the city at all cost, and so it was determined to attack the boom. Why it was not attacked weeks before remains a mystery, but at any rate, now the attempt was to be made. Among the merchant ships that accompanied Kirke's fleet were two, named the " Mountjoy," commanded by Captain Browning, a native of Londonderry, and the " Phœnix," whose master was Captain Douglas. Both these vessels were laden with provisions, and now these two men volunteered to lead the attack.

" It was July 28th. The sun had just set ; the evening sermon in the cathedral was over, and the heartbroken congregation had separated, when the sentinels on the tower saw the sails of three vessels coming up the Foyle. Soon there was a stir in the Irish camp. The besiegers were on the alert for miles along both shores. The ships were in extreme peril, for the river was low, and the only navigable channel ran very near to the left bank, where the headquarters of the enemy had been fixed, and where the batteries were most numerous. Leake (the captain of the man-of-war accompanying the two merchantmen) performed his duty with a skill and spirit worthy of his noble profession, exposed his frigate to cover the merchantmen, and used his guns with great effect. At length the little squadron came to the place of peril. Then the "Mountjoy" took the lead, and went right at the boom. The huge barricade cracked and gave way; but the shock was such that the "Mountjoy" rebounded, and stuck in the mud. A yell of triumph rose from the banks; the Irish rushed to their boats, and were preparing to board, but the "Dartmouth" (Captain Leake's vessel) poured on them a well directed broadside, which threw them into disorder. Just then the "Phœnix" dashed at the breach which the "Mountjoy" had made, and was in a moment within the fence. Meantime the tide was rising fast. The "Mountjoy" began to move, and soon passed safe through the broken stakes and floating spars. But her brave master was no more. A shot from one of the batteries had struck him, and he died by the most enviable of all deaths, in sight of the city which was his birthplace, which was his home, and which had just been saved by his courage and self-devotion from the most frightful form of destruction. The night had closed in before the conflict at the boom

"Starving multitudes were there to welcome them."

began, but the flash of the guns was seen, and
the noise heard, by the lean and ghastly
multitude which covered the walls of the city.
When the "Mountjoy" grounded, and when
the shout of triumph rose from the Irish on both
sides of the river, the hearts of the besieged
died within them. One who endured the
unutterable anguish of that moment has told
us that they looked fearfully livid in each
other's eyes. Even after the barricade had
been passed, there was a terrible half-hour of
suspense. It was ten o'clock before the ships
arrived at the quay. The whole population
was there to welcome them. A screen made
of casks filled with earth, was hastily thrown
up to protect the landing place from the
batteries on the other side of the river; and
then the work of unloading began. First, were
rolled on shore, barrels containing six thousand
bushels of meal. Then came great cheeses,
casks of beef, flitches of bacon, kegs of butter,
sacks of peas and biscuit, ankers of brandy.
Not many hours before, half a pound of tallow
and three quarters of a pound of salted hide
had been weighed out with niggardly care to
every fighting man. The ration which each
now received was three pounds of flour, two
pounds of beef, and a pint of peas. It is easy
to imagine with what tears grace was said over
the suppers of that evening. There was little
sleep on either side of the wall. The bonfires
shone bright along the whole circuit of the
ramparts. The Irish guns continued to roar
all night; and all night the bells of the rescued

city made answer to the Irish guns with a peal
of joyous defiance. Through the three following days the batteries of the enemy continued
to play. But, on the third night, flames were
seen arising from the camp; and when the
first of August dawned, a line of smoking ruins
marked the site lately occupied by the huts of
the besiegers ; and the citizens saw, far off, the
long column of spikes and standards retreating
up the left bank of the Foyle towards
Strabane."*

Thus ended this memorable siege, and to-
day Protestants should remember with deep
gratitude, the God-given courage that animated
the brave defenders of Londonderry. Had
they given in, most likely the history of the
last two centuries would have been very
different. Those noble men not only saved
Ireland from being entirely subjected to
Popery, but the safety and Protestantism of
England itself was at stake, and the Protestant
King William III. might never have been
established on the throne had not Londonderry held out right nobly in those brave
days of old.

In due course William III. landed with an
army on the shores of Ireland, and after the
decisive battle of the Boyne James II.
decamped, but it was the 'prentice boys of
Derry who saved the situation.

---

* Lord Macaulay.

"Barrels of meal, great cheeses, casks of beef, and provisions of all sorts were landed on the quay."

CHAPTER VI

A VISIT TO LONDONDERRY OF THE EARLY 1900'S

———

THE writer deemed it worth his while to undertake a long journey by land and sea in order to visit the famous city of Londonderry, whose story shines out so brightly on the pages of Protestant history. It is now a busy seaport, covering a far greater area than it did in the dreadful days of 1688-89, but it is a comparatively easy matter to imagine the size and appearance of the city in those days. The walls that were so despised by the French and the Irish are still there. Some of the cannon that belched forth such unanswerable arguments still show their grim muzzles through apertures in the ramparts, among them being "Roaring Meg," the biggest gun possessed by the besieged, which holds the place of honour among the relics of that terrible time of suffering. Few more interesting walks can be imagined than a tour around the walls, and the writer confesses that it is difficult to express what were his feelings as he stood at the foot of the monument which has been erected to the memory of the Rev. George Walker, the heroic governor of Derry. It rears its head ninety feet above the walls of the city. On its summit is a colossal figure of Walker; in his right hand he holds a Bible, in his left there was originally a sword pointing in the direction of the river, but, many years ago, the sword, owing to the continued action of the wind in so exposed a position, fell to the ground, and was never replaced. The pillar was erected in 1827-28, at a cost of four thousand two hundred pounds, raised by public subscription. Hard by the monument is the cathedral, which bore such a conspicuous and prominent place in the story of the siege. It has been restored in recent years, but it still bears the general semblance of what it was in 1688. In the churchyard there is a large mound, and on it an obelisk bearing the following inscription:—" To the memory and in honour of the illustrious men who distinguished themselves in the siege of Derry, 1688-89, and of other eminent citizens whose bodies, interred within the cathedral before, during, and after that memorable event, were exhumed in 1861 during the alterations of the building. The 'prentice boys, aided by Harvey Nicholson, Esq., and other friends, having collected the bones, reverently reinterred them on the north side of the cathedral on the 24th day of May, 1861, and

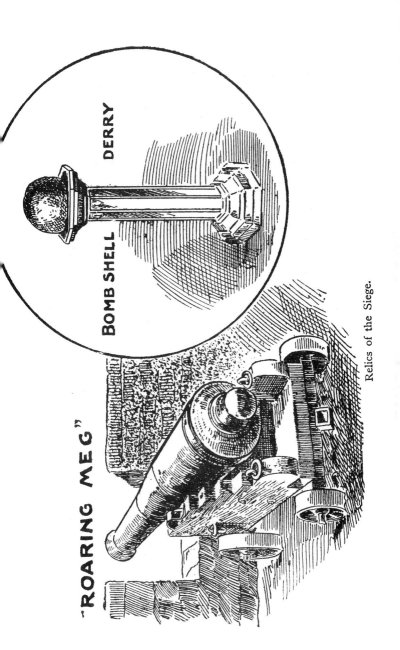

"ROARING MEG"

BOMB SHELL

DERRY

Relics of the Siege.

erected this mound composed of their earthly remains."

> "That hallowed graveyard yonder
> Swells with the soldier dead ;
> Oh, brothers, pause and ponder,
> It was for US they bled."

As one stands on the walls of Derry it is very easy to note the advantages the besiegers had over those within the city, for lofty hills look down on Londonderry on all sides, with the exception, of course, of that part of the city which faces Lough Foyle. Its blue waters still glisten in the sunshine, as they must have done in 1689, appearing to mock the inhabitants when they knew that a few miles off upon its bosom were the abundant supplies which they so much needed. The present inhabitants of Derry are proud of the part which their city played in the conflict of 1688, and they annually commemorate the relief of the city, and annually, too, execrate the memory of the traitor, Colonel Lundy, by burning him in effigy.

Among the many other things to be noticed in this famous city are the city arms, which are here reproduced. On it appears the arms of the City of London, and the reason of their incorporation into the arms of the Irish city is explained on a quaint tablet to be found in the cathedral, on which it states that—

> "If stones could speake then London's prayse should sound,
> Who built this church and cittie from the ground."

The most striking thing about the arms, however, is the gaunt skeleton that occupies a portion of the lower half of the design, indicating the suffering endured during the famous siege. The motto " *Vita veritas victoria*," strikes a note of triumph that well deserves a community that has suffered so nobly in the cause of truth and freedom.

The City Arms.

To all who contemplate an enjoyable holiday jaunt the writer can recommend the famous city, for the country around is very charming, and the excursions both by sea and land are most interesting and attractive. But if during their stay my readers should experience wet weather—for it knows how to rain in a very business-like way in Ireland—they cannot spend their time more profitably than by committing to memory the following beautiful poem, by Mrs. C. F. Alexander, inserted by permission of the proprietors of the *National Review* :—

THE SIEGE OF DERRY.

By Mrs. C. F. Alexander.

" Oh, my daughter ! lead me forth to the bastion on the north,
　Let me see the water running from the green hills of Tyrone,
Where the woods of ' Mountjoy ' quiver above the changeful river,
　And the silver trout lies hidden in the pools that I have known.

" There I wooed your mother, dear ! in the days that are so near
　To the old man who lies dying in this sore beleaguered place ;
For time's long years may sever, but love, that liveth ever,
　Calls back the early rapture—lights again the angel face.

" Ah, well ! she lieth still on our well engirdled hill,
　Our own cathedral holds her till God shall call His dead ;
And the psalter's swell and wailing, and the cannon's loud assailing,
　And the preacher's voice and blessing, pass unheeded o'er her head.

" 'Twas the Lord who gave the word when His people drew the sword
　For the freedom of the present, for the future that awaits.
Oh, child ! thou must remember that bleak day in December
　When the 'prentice boys of Derry rose up and shut the gates.

" There was tumult in the street, and a rush of many feet—
　There was discord in the Council, and Lundy turned to fly :
For the man had no assurance of Ulstermen's endurance,
　Nor the strength of him who trusted in the arm of God Most High.

" These limbs, that now are weak, were strong then, and thy cheek
　Held roses that were red as any rose in June—
That now are wan, my daughter ! as the light on the Foyle water,
　When all the sea and all the land are white beneath the moon.

" Then the foemen gathered fast—we could see them marching past—
　The Irish from his barren hills, the Frenchman from his wars,
With their banners bravely beaming, and to our eyes their seeming
　Was fearful as a locust band, and countless as the stars.

" And they bound us with a cord from the harbour to the ford,
    And they raked us with their cannon, and sallying was hot ;
But our trust was still unshaken, though Culmore Fort was taken,
    And they wrote our men a letter, and they sent it in a shot.

" They were soft words that they spoke, how we need not fear
        their yoke,
    And they pleaded by our homesteads, and by our children small,
And our women fair and tender; but we answer'd, ' No surrender ! '
    And we called on God Almighty, and we went to man the wall.

" There was wrath in the French camp ; we could hear their
        captain stamp,
    And Rosen, with his hand on his cross'd hilt, swore
That little town of Derry, not a league from Culmore ferry,
    Should lie a heap of ashes on the Foyle's green shore.

" Like a falcon on her perch, our fair cathedral church
    Above the tide-vext river looks eastward from the bay—
Dear namesake of St. Columb, and each morning sweet and
        solemn,
    The bells, through all the tumult, have call'd us in to pray.

" Our leader speaks the prayer—the captains all are there—
    His deep voice never falters, though his look be sad and grave,
On the women's pallid faces, and the soldiers in their places,
    And the stones above our brothers that lie buried in the nave.

" They are closing round us still by the river ; on the hill
    You can see the white pavilions round the standard of their
        chief ;
But the Lord is up in heaven, though the chances are uneven,
    Though the boom is in the river whence we look'd for our relief.

" And the faint hope dies away at the close of each long day,
    As we see the eyes grow lustreless, the pulses beating low ;
As we see our children languish—was ever martyr's anguish,
    At the stake or in the dungeon, like this anguish that we know ?

" With the foemen's closing line, while the English make no sign,
    And the daily lessening ration, and the fall of staggering feet,
And the wailing low and fearful, and the women stern and tearful,
    Speaking bravely to their husbands and their lovers in the street.

" There was trouble in the air when we met this day for prayer,
    And the joyous July morning was heavy in our eyes ;
Our arms were by the altar as we sang aloud the Psalter,
    And listened in the pauses for the enemy's surprise.

" ' Praise the Lord God in the height, for the glory of His might ! '
    It ran along the arches and it went out to the town :
' In His strength He hath risen, He hath loos'd the souls in prison,
    The wrong'd one He hath righted, and raised the fallen-down.'

" And the preacher's voice was bold, as he rose up then and told
   Of the triumphs of the righteous, of the patience of the saints,
And the hope of God's assistance, and the greatness of resistance,
   Of the trust that never wearies and the heart that never faints.

      *   *   *   *   *   *

" Where the river joins the brine canst thou see the ships in line ?
   And the plenty of our craving, just beyond the cruel boom ?
Through the dark mist of the firing canst thou see the masts
     aspiring ?
   Dost thou think of one who loves thee on that ship amidst the
     gloom ? "

She was weary, she was wan, but she climbed the rampart on,
   And she looked along the water, where the good ships lay
     afar—
" Oh ! I see on either border their cannon ranged in order,
   And the boom across the river, and the waiting men-of-war.

" There's death in every hand that holds a lighted brand,
   But the gallant little 'Mountjoy' comes bravely to the front.
Now, God of Battles, hear us ! let that good ship draw near us.
   Ah ! the brands are at the touch-holes—will she bear the
     cannon's brunt ?

" She makes a forward dash. Hark, hark ! the thunder crash !
   Oh, Father, they have caught her—she is lying on the shore.
Another crash like thunder—will it tear her ribs asunder ?
   No, no ! the shot has freed her—she is floating on once
     more.

" She pushes her white sail through the bullets' leaden hail,
   Now blessings on her captain and on her seamen bold.
Crash ! crash ! the boom is broken : I can see my true love's
    token—
A lily in his bonnet, a lily all of gold.

" She sails up to the town, like a queen in a white gown ;
   Red golden are her lilies, true gold are all her men.
Now the 'Phœnix' follows after—I can hear the women's
    láughter,
   And the shouting of the soldiers, till the echoes ring again."

She has glided from the wall, on her lover's breast to fall,
   As the white bird of the ocean drops down into the wave ;
And the bells are madly ringing, and a hundred voices singing,
   And the old man on the bastion has joined the triumph stave.

" Sing ye praises through the land : the Lord with His right hand,
   With His mighty arm hath gotten Himself the victory now.
He hath scattered their forces, both the rider and their horses.
   There is none that fighteth for us, O God ! but only Thou."

And of these heroic times, if the tale be told in rhymes,
  When the statesman of the future learns no lesson from the
    past ;
When rude hands are upsetting, and cold hearts are forgetting,
  And faction sways the senate, and faith is overcast :

Then these Derry men shall tell—who would serve his country
    well,
  Must be strong in his conviction and valiant in his deed,
Must be patient in enduring, and determined in securing
  The liberty to serve his God, the freedom of his creed.

Londonderry 1986.